## SCIENCE ANSWERS

# Forces and Motion

### FROM PUSH TO SHOVE

Heinemann Library
Chicago, Illinois

## Christopher Cooper

Design: Jo Hinton-Malivoire and
  Tinstar Design Ltd (www.tinstar.co.uk)
Illustrations: Jeff Edwards
Picture Research: Rosie Garai and Liz
  Eddison
Originated by Dot Gradations Ltd.
Printed and bound in the United States by
Lake Book Manufacturing, Inc.
08 07
10 9 8 7 6

**Library of Congress Cataloging-in-Publication Data**
Cooper, Christopher (Christopher Robin),
1944-
   Forces and motion : from push to shove /
Christopher Cooper.
      v. cm. -- (Science answers)
Includes bibliographical references and
index.
Contents: What are forces? -- What
happens when you push or pull an
object? -- How can forces change the shape
of objects? -- How can you make objects
move faster and slower? -- Why do things
fall to the ground when you drop them? --
Why do some things float? -- What is
pressure? --How can forces work for us?
   ISBN 1-4034-0951-X (HC), 1-4034-3548-0
(pbk.)
   1.  Force and energy--Juvenile literature. 2.
Motion--Juvenile
literature. [1. Force and energy. 2. Motion.]
I. Title. II. Series.
   QC73.4.C66 2003
   531'.6--dc21

**Acknowledgments**
The author and publishers are grateful to
the following for permission to reproduce
copyright material:

p. 4 Hughes Martin/Corbis; p.5 Arthur
Tilley/Getty Images; Douglas
Peebles/Corbis; pp. 8, 12, 25 Trevor
Clifford; p.9 George D. Lepp/Corbis; p. 11
Orban Thierry/Corbis; p.13 Tom
Stewar/Corbis; p. 14 Takeshi
Takahara/Science Photo Library; pp. 17, 18
Science Photo Library; p. 20 Robert Y.
Kaufman/Corbis; p. 21 Joel W.
Rogers/Corbis; p. 22 Tudor Photography;
p. 23 Jack Ambrose/Getty Images; p. 26
Nigel Rolstone/Corbis; p. 28
Bettman/Corbis; p. 29 Corbis.

Cover photograph reproduced with
permission of Corbis/David Stoecklern.

Every effort has been made to contact
copyright holders of any material
reproduced in this book. Any omissions
will be rectified in subsequent printings
if notice is given to the publishers.

Some words are shown in
bold, **like this.** You can find
out what they mean by
looking in the glossary.

ISBN 978-1-4034-0951-5 (1-4034-0951-X) (HC)
ISBN 978-1-4034-3548-4 (1-4034-3548-0 ) (Pbk.)

2003002503

# Contents

## About the experiments and demonstrations

In each chapter of this book you will find a section called Science Answers. It describes an experiment or demonstration that you can try yourself. There are some simple safety rules to follow when doing an experiment:

- Ask an adult to help with any cutting using a sharp knife.
- Electricity is dangerous. Never, ever try to experiment with it.
- Do not use any of your experimental **materials** near an electrical socket.

## Materials you will use

Most of the experiments and demonstrations in this book can be done with objects you can find in your own home. A few will need items you can buy from a hardware store. You will also need paper and a pencil to record your results.

# What Are Forces?

A **force** is a push or a pull. There are many ways that objects can be pushed or pulled. The world is full of movements caused by forces. Your bicycle rolls downhill unless you press the brake. When you press the brake, it slows the bicycle down. When you hit a ball with a tennis racket, the ball starts moving or, if it is already moving, changes direction. Cars and airplanes use powerful engines to push them forward and up into the sky.

There are other kinds of movements. The sky, the air, and the sea are never still. Even the ground under your feet is **constantly** moving. Everything around you is made up of tiny particles called **atoms.** Even the smallest grain of sand is made up of millions of atoms that are constantly in motion. The chair on which you sit may seem perfectly still, but it is made up of atoms that **vibrate** all the time.

## Sliding downhill

The force of **gravity** affects everything on Earth. Gravity makes this skier slide downhill. The snow is slippery, so when the skier starts moving, the snow exerts only weak **friction,** a type of force between objects. The force of gravity is stronger than the forces slowing the skis, so the skier goes faster and faster. As the skier travels faster, the force exerted by the snow increases. When the snow's force equals the force of gravity, the skier travels at a constant, high speed.

### Exerting a force

Whenever an object **speeds** up, slows down, or starts moving in a different direction, it is because a **force** has acted on it.

People say that a force is **exerted** when something moves. You exert a force whenever you pick something up, throw it, or push it, or pull it.

## Kicking a ball

This boy exerts a force on the ball by kicking it. The ball will change direction when it is kicked. The harder the ball is kicked, the more quickly it will travel in the new direction. The wind exerts a force on the ball when it is in the air. The ground exerts a force on the ball when it lands.

# What Happens When You Push or Pull an Object?

You can see the effects of **forces** whenever you push something. If you push a shopping cart it moves away from you. If you pull the shopping cart, it moves toward you.

The muscles of your body are **exerting** a force, and the object being pushed or pulled is responding to that force.

## Opposing forces

Exerting a force, however, does not always make something move. This is because there is nearly always more than one force acting on any object. For example, if you try to push or pull a heavy block of concrete lying on the ground, it will probably not move at all. This is because there is a lot of **friction** between the block and the ground. Friction is the force created whenever two objects rub against one another. In order to move the block, your push or pull force would have to be greater than the friction force between the block and the ground.

The amount of friction between two materials depends on how strongly they are pressed together. The heavy block of concrete presses strongly on the ground and creates a strong friction force. A smaller, lighter block would press less strongly and create a weaker friction force. The amount of friction also depends on what two types of material are being pressed together. The heavy block of concrete resting on ice would slide more easily because ice is very smooth.

The scientist Isaac Newton came up with some rules that describe forces and their effects. His first rule is called **Newton's first law of motion.** It says that an object will stay still or continue moving in the same direction at the same **speed** unless a force is applied to it. When you push a shopping cart you are applying force to it, causing it to move. If you let go, it would keep moving in the same direction at the same speed, except that friction between the wheels and the ground would slow it down or cause it to change direction.

## Forces in nature

These boats are being pushed along by the wind. The wind is exerting a force on the sails of the boats, and that force is greater than the friction of the boats on the water. The boats would stop moving if they accidentally ran onto the beach. The force of the friction on land would be stronger than the force of the wind. The water causes less friction, because it can flow and so gets out of the way of the boats.

# EXPERIMENT: How can you move objects around more easily?

## HYPOTHESIS

If the amount of **friction** between objects is reduced, they should move more easily.

## EQUIPMENT

A length of string about 24 inches (60 centimeters) long, a wide rubber band about 4 inches (10 centimeters) long, a medium-sized book or similar-size object, a packet of straight plastic drinking straws

## EXPERIMENT STEPS

1. Pass the string through the rubber band. Tie the ends of the string together.
2. Place the book on a tabletop and loop the string around the book so that you can pull the book along.
3. Hold the rubber band and pull the book across the table. Try to keep it moving steadily. Notice how much the rubber band stretches. The more force that is needed to pull the book, the more the rubber band will stretch.
4. Now make a road of straws. In the same way as before, drag the book along this road, with the straws acting as rollers. Does the rubber band stretch more or less than before?
5. Write down what you saw.

   *(See the next page for the conclusion.)*

**CONCLUSION**

You should have found that the rubber band stretched less when the book moved on the straw rollers. There is less friction because the book and the straws do not rub against each other. The rolling straws move with the book. Large rollers are sometimes used to move heavy objects.

## A heavy load

It takes a big force from the locomotive to get these heavy freight cars moving. But once the train is moving, it needs a very strong force to make it stop. Trains like this have to have good brakes to apply that force.

# How Can Forces Change the Shape of Objects?

**Forces** affect different materials in very different ways. A material's **reaction** to a force depends on how the material **resists** or reacts to the applied force. If you push your finger into a piece of modeling clay, the clay hardly resists at all and is pushed aside. When you pull your finger away, the clay does not go back to its original shape. It stays in its new shape. This is because the **atoms** in the clay are not held **rigidly** in place by strong chemical links.

The atoms in a hard material such as wood are held together by strong chemical links that keep them rigidly in place. There is almost no change of shape when you apply a weak force to a piece of wood. If you apply a very strong force, the wood might shatter.

## What makes things bouncy?

Rubber and many plastics are **elastic.** When you stretch or squeeze them, their shape changes. At the same time, they pull or push back. Thus, as you pull on a rubber band, it becomes harder and harder to stretch it the longer it gets. When you release the force (the pull), an elastic material bounces, or springs, back into its original shape.

Elastic materials behave as if their atoms are linked by springs. When the material is stretched or squeezed, the springs try to return to their original length and bring the atoms back to their original positions. It is similar to a trampoline, in which the bouncy surface is supported by springs. The springs always try to pull the surface back into its flat shape.

## Springing back into shape

The material in a tennis ball is elastic. When it is hit hard, the ball is squashed, but it springs back into shape as it leaves the racket.

 **• SCIENCE ANSWERS •**

## EXPERIMENT: What makes some balls bouncier than others?

### HYPOTHESIS
Balls will be more or less bouncy, depending on whether they are made of plastic or latex, on whether they are solid or have air in the middle, and on how heavy they are.

### EQUIPMENT
Ruler or tape measure, a wall that you can temporarily mark with pencil or chalk, bouncy balls made of several different materials (a tennis ball, a Ping-Pong ball, and various balls from a toy store, including a super-bouncy ball), a person to help you

*(Continued on the next page.)*

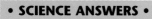 

## EXPERIMENT STEPS

1. Make a mark about shoulder height on the wall.
2. Arrange the balls into groups so that all the balls in each group are about the same size.
3. Drop each ball in turn from the mark on the wall. Make sure you simply drop it and not throw it, otherwise you will apply extra force to the ball.
4. Have the other person mark the height that the ball rises to on its first bounce. The more **elastic** the ball is, the higher it will bounce.
5. For each group of balls, make a note of the type of ball and the height each reached. Was the ball hollow? Did it have a solid core? Was it made from hard plastic or soft rubber?
6. Write down what you saw.

## CONCLUSION

No ball is perfectly elastic. None of them rises to the same height that it was dropped from. But some do rise higher than others.

Now clean the marks off the wall!

# How Can You Make Objects Move Faster and Slower?

If there were no **forces** acting on it, an object would keep on going at the same **speed**—forever! This is because, according to Isaac **Newton's first law of motion,** an object continues at rest or moving at **constant** speed in a straight line unless acted on by an outside force.

However, when a force is applied to an object, as long as there is not an equal and opposite force, it will make the object go faster or slower. Or, it will change its direction. This is **Newton's second law of motion.**

### What do action and reaction mean?

Isaac **Newton's third law of motion** states:

*For every action there is an equal and opposite reaction.*

**Action** simply is a force. A **reaction** is an opposing force that is supplied by another action. When you press down on a tabletop, the force you press down with is the action. The table presses back upward— otherwise your hand would keep going down. That upward force by the table is the reaction.

## Why does everything need a force to keep it moving?

Without a force to keep it moving, an object can be slowed or stopped by other forces, including **friction** and **gravity.** A car or truck rolls to a halt if the engine is turned off because of friction with the road. A bicycle comes to a stop when you stop pedaling because of friction with the road surface. A rocket starts to slow down when its engines stop firing because of the gravitational pull of Earth.

# What a drag!

When a car is moving, it experiences a strong **force** holding it back. This is caused by the air rushing past it. This slowing force is called drag. Engineers study the drag on a new car design by putting the car, or a model of the car, in a wind tunnel. They measure the force that acts on the car when a strong stream of air blows over it.

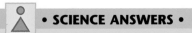 

# EXPERIMENT: Is Newton's third law of motion correct?

## HYPOTHESIS
For every **action** there is an equal and opposite **reaction.**

## EQUIPMENT
Modeling clay, four drinking straws (two different sizes and thicknesses), a large plastic drink bottle, heavy paper, sticky tape

## EXPERIMENT STEPS
1. Place a ball of modeling clay large enough to cover the mouth of the bottle around one end of one of the smaller straws.
2. Place this end of the straw and the clay just inside the bottle so that the clay blocks the mouth of the bottle.
3. Cut two strips of the heavy paper. One should be 5.5 inches (14 centimeters) long and 1 inch (2.5 centimeters) wide; the other piece needs to be 3 inches (7 centimeters) long and 1 inch (2.5 centimeters) wide.
4. Form the two pieces of paper into circles (see picture).
5. Tape the largest circle on the base of a larger straw so that it looks like it forms a hoop around the straw.
6. Tape the smaller circle at the end of the large straw. Support the straws by holding the hoops.
7. Put a small ball of clay into the end of the large straw.
8. Insert the small straw that is attached to the bottle inside the large straw. Squeeze the bottle and see what happens.
9. Write down what you saw.

## CONCLUSION
When you squeeze the plastic bottle, the air inside is blown through the small straw and into the larger straw. Since the air cannot escape through the plugged end of the large straw, **pressure** builds up and makes the straw shoot forward. This proves **Newton's third law of motion**: For every action there is an equal and opposite reaction.

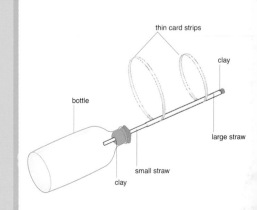

thin card strips

clay

bottle

large straw

small straw

clay

# Why Do Things Fall to the Ground When You Drop Them?

Everything near the earth tends to fall to the ground unless something prevents it. This tendency is called **gravity.** An object falls to the ground because of a downward **force** called its **weight.** Weight is called a gravitational force. It is greater for a heavy object and less for a lighter object. A brick has more weight than a cotton ball.

Gravity keeps you from falling off Earth and floating into space. It also makes water run downhill.

### Is everything affected by gravity?

All objects, in space and on the earth, are attracted to each other by gravity. The moon, planets, sun, and stars all have gravity that pulls things toward them.

You can see and feel the effects of Earth's gravity. You see things fall as they are pulled down by gravity. When you carry something, you can feel its weight, which is the result of gravity. You can feel the pull of Earth on you, too, when you sit on a chair and feel the **pressure** of the furniture against your body.

### How strong is gravity?

The strength of the gravitational force is different between different objects. It depends on the **masses** of the objects. An eighteen-wheeled truck contains much more mass than you do. So the pull of Earth's gravity on it is much greater than gravity's pull on you. This is just another way of saying that the truck is much heavier than you are.

The strength of the gravitational force also depends on the distance between objects. When they are farther away from each other, the force is weaker. If you were an astronaut floating in space, as far away from Earth as the Moon is, Earth's gravitational tug on you would be less than a thousandth of what it now is.

## Escaping gravity

An object that is trying to travel into space needs to have very powerful engines. But even the engines on this space shuttle do not enable it to escape the force of Earth's gravity completely. Instead, it stays in a circular path, or orbit, around Earth.

## Earth, the Sun, and the Moon

**Gravity** is the reason why Earth goes around the Sun. It is also the reason why the Moon goes around Earth. The Moon has much less **mass** than Earth does, so its gravitational force is less.

Astronauts who land on the Moon feel lighter. The amount of **matter** in their bodies, or their mass, is the same as on Earth. However, the effect of gravity on that mass—that is, their weight—is smaller.

# Why Do Things Float?

In a tub of water, each drop of water is held in place by the **pressure,** or pushing **force,** of all the drops of water around it. There are sideways, downward, and upward pushes, combining to give an upward force. This force balances the **weight** of that drop of water exactly, keeping it in place.

## What is displacement?

When you place a piece of wood gently in a container that is filled to the top with water, some of the water overflows. The water is **displaced** by the piece of wood.

After the displaced water has spilled out of the container, the water that remains pushes the object in the same way that it previously pushed on the water that was displaced. So there is an upward force on the object equal to the weight of the displaced water.

The wood is less **dense** than water. Its weight is less than the weight of an equal **volume** of water. So the weight of the wood is less than the upthrust that it now "feels." The wood moves upward, or floats.

## Archimedes' principle

This can be summed up in Archimedes' principle, which is named after the Greek scientist who first discovered it more than 2,000 years ago. He studied liquids, but his theory applies to all fluids, or materials that flow:

*The upward force on an object in a fluid is equal to the weight of the displaced fluid.*

## How do submarines work?

Submarines have large tanks that are filled partly with water and partly with air. When the submarine needs to dive, air is pumped out of the tanks, which then take in more water. Air is much less **dense** than water, so replacing some of the air with water makes the submarine as a whole more dense. In other words, the submarine becomes heavier and sinks beneath the surface.

To get back to the surface quickly, compressed air (air that is under greater pressure than you find in the atmosphere) stored onboard the submarine is blown into the tank. This pushes water out and makes the submarine less heavy, so it rises.

# Can an object made of heavy iron float?

Iron is denser than water. This means that a piece of iron weighs more than the same **volume** of water. If you put a solid piece of iron into the water, the upward push is not enough to keep it at the surface.

But if the iron is a hollow shape, like a bowl, the **density** of the iron bowl now includes the air inside it. Air, of course, is less dense than water. Ships built from dense iron and steel float because there is so much air inside them.

# EXPERIMENT: How can you make an object float and sink in water?

## HYPOTHESIS

An object may float if it **displaces** more water, and sink if it displaces less.

## EQUIPMENT

A large plastic drink bottle with a cap, a bowl, a large pen cap, several paper clips

## EXPERIMENT STEPS

1. Fill a bowl with water. Attach the paper clips around the opening of the pen cap until it will just about float upright in the bowl, trapping an air bubble.
2. Fill the bottle nearly to the top with water and float the paper clipped pen cap in it. Screw on the bottle cap.
3. Now squeeze the bottle: The submarine pen cap will sink to the bottom. Release the bottle and it floats to the surface.

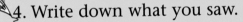

4. Write down what you saw.

## CONCLUSION

Squeezing the bottle means you are **exerting** pressure on the water inside—you are pushing on the water. The water in turn exerts pressure on the air bubble, making it smaller in the pen cap. This means that the air bubble displaces less water and there is less of an upward **force** on the bubble. So the pen cap submarine sinks.

# What Is Pressure?

The air around you is like a mixture of different gases, such as oxygen and carbon dioxide. These gases make up Earth's atmosphere. The gases in air have **weight** and press on you and everything around you. They push you from all directions. This push is called **pressure.**

Air is much less **dense** than the same **volume** of water. But the atmosphere is hundreds of miles thick. The column of air above a square foot (0.1 square meter) of Earth's surface has a **mass** of more than ten tons.

## What is the pressure at the bottom of the ocean?

As you go deeper in the ocean, there is more water on top of you. More water weighs more. This means the water pressure increases. This diver's suit contains air. It has added pressure that pushes back against the water pressure of the ocean. But not even the most advanced diver's suit would enable anyone to go to the bottom of the deepest parts of the Pacific Ocean. The sea floor there is 6 miles (10 kilometers) deep and the pressure is 1,000 times the atmospheric pressure at the surface.

# DEMONSTRATION: Crushing proof

Air **pressure** increases when the air is heated. You can prove this yourself by following the steps below.

## EQUIPMENT

An empty plastic drink bottle with a cap, hot water *(Warning: Do not use boiling or very hot water from a faucet, which is dangerous and may melt the plastic bottle.)*

## DEMONSTRATION STEPS:

1. Half-fill the bottle with hot water. Screw on the cap.
2. Shake up the bottle to warm up the air inside and mix it with water vapor (water in gas form).
3. Pour out the liquid and quickly screw the cap back on.
4. Now run cold water from the tap over the bottle. As the air inside cools, and the water vapor turns back into liquid water, the bottle is squashed and crumples.
5. Write down what you saw.

## EXPLANATION

The hot air and water vapor were at a higher pressure than the cold air and water. As the contents of the bottle were cooled, the pressure inside the bottle fell. The pressure of the air and water vapor inside no longer balanced the pressure of the air outside. Therefore, the bottle was squashed.

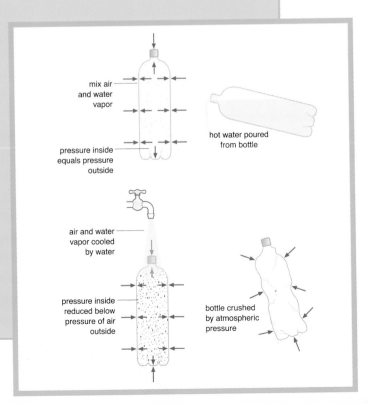

mix air and water vapor

pressure inside equals pressure outside

hot water poured from bottle

air and water vapor cooled by water

pressure inside reduced below pressure of air outside

bottle crushed by atmospheric pressure

# How Can Forces Work for You?

The term *simple machine* has a special meaning to scientists. It is a **device** that changes the direction of a **force,** its strength, or the place where the force is applied.

A simple machine can be an everyday device such as a **lever.** An example of a lever is a crowbar. You push downward on one end of a crowbar and the other end rises, lifting, for example, a large, flat stone. Your push is called the **effort.** The **weight** of the stone is called the **load.**

There are other kinds of simple machines that do not use levers. For example, **pulleys** are often used in industry. These are arrangements of wheels and cables that increase the pulling power of engines and human muscles.

## How can a person lift a car?

One type of car jack uses a handle that a person turns. Every time the handle turns, the car is raised a little. After many turns the effort, or the force applied by the person, has moved a long way, while the load—the heavy car—has risen only a short way.

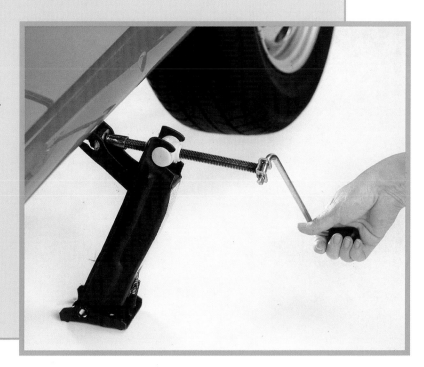

## How do simple machines work?

**Simple machines** are usually, although not always, used to increase the strength of the **force** that the user **exerts**. In these cases, the machines are designed so that the **effort** moves farther than the **load.** This is the secret of the simple machine: A small effort moving a long way can result in a large load moving a small distance.

### A big haul

The winch, a machine that coils a rope, on this boat is being used to pull in a rope. The rope is holding the sail. **Friction** holds the rope on the drum of the winch. The person using the winch uses a handle as a **lever** to turn the drum.

# EXPERIMENT: How can one person overcome the strength of several people?

## HYPOTHESIS
A simple machine can be rigged up to increase the force exerted by a single person.

## EQUIPMENT
Two broomsticks, rakes, or similar poles; a length of rope at least 20 feet (6 meters) long; the assistance of several people

## EXPERIMENT STEPS
1. Lay the poles next to each other on the ground, about 12 inches (30 centimeters) apart.
2. Tie the rope to the end of one of the poles.
3. Loop the rope back and forth at least six times over the two poles as shown. The rope now makes a zigzag between the poles.
4. Take the free end of the rope, while the other people pick up the poles.
5. Pull on the rope as hard as you can while your opponents try as hard as they can to pull the poles apart.
6. Write down what you saw.

## CONCLUSION
If the rope is looped around the poles enough times, you can defeat several adults. The secret is that the effort, or the force you apply, moves much farther than the load, or the force your opponents apply.

knot

# People Who Found the Answers

### Archimedes of Syracuse (287-212 B.C.E.)

Archimedes of Syracuse was possibly the greatest scientist of the ancient world. He made many mathematical discoveries and studied **forces** and movement. In what is now called Archimedes' principle, he stated that a body in a liquid experiences an upward force equal to the **weight** of the liquid **displaced.**

Archimedes is said to have invented tools and weapons of war to defend his home city of Syracuse against Roman armies. They included cranes that lifted whole ships out of the water and huge mirrors that reflected sunlight onto ships and set fire to their sails.

### Isaac Newton (1642-1727 C.E.)

Isaac Newton founded the modern understanding of force. He studied at the University of Cambridge in England until 1665, when there was an outbreak of disease. He had to go home for a while. The story goes that while home, he saw an apple fall from a tree. He had the idea that the same force that pulled it to the ground was keeping the Moon moving around Earth. This went against the long-held idea that the planets obey completely different laws from those that hold on Earth.

Newton went further in his law of universal **gravitation.** This states that every piece of **matter** in the universe attracts every other piece. He also discovered the three laws of motion. With these and other discoveries, Newton was able to explain the movements of falling objects and of the Moon and planets, as well as the rise and fall of tides.

# Amazing Facts

- All forces are produced by four fundamental, or basic, forces. **Gravity** is one fundamental force. Electromagnetism is another—sometimes electromagnetism appears as electric forces, at other times as magnetic forces. Two fundamental forces, called the strong and the weak nuclear forces, operate in the center of an **atom.** The strongest fundamental force is the nuclear force and the weakest is gravity.

- Atoms can be photographed with a microscope that measures forces instead of by focusing light. The atomic force microscope (AFM) contains a tiny strip of springy material. The strip is moved across the surface of a sample being studied, about a millionth of an inch away from the surface. The surface attracts the strip more strongly where the gap between them is smaller because the surface is uneven. The tiny force at each point is measured. A computer turns this information into a picture of the surface.

- The greatest amount of controlled force produced by people is developed by the space shuttle. At launch, two solid-fuel booster rockets generate about 1,543 tons of thrust each. A force of 1 ton is equal to the weight of an object that has a **mass** of 1 ton. In addition, there are three main engines burning, each generating about 187 tons of force. That adds up to more than 3,300 tons of force.

# Glossary

**action** force—for every action there is an equal force in the opposite direction called the reaction

**atom** tiny particles from which matter is made. It consists of still smaller particles.

**constant** always the same

**dense** very heavy

**density** how heavy an object is for its size

**device** something made for a special purpose

**displaced** pushed aside. An object placed in liquid displaces some of the liquid.

**effort** force exerted by a person, an animal, or a machine to make something move

**elastic** able to stretch and go back to the same shape after having been pulled or squeezed out of shape

**exert** make, give, or produce a force

**force** a push or a pull that moves an object or changes its direction

**friction** force of attraction between atoms that tends to stop two objects or materials from moving when they are in contact with each other

**gravity** force of attraction between every particle in the universe and every other particle. Also called gravitation.

**lever** device consisting of a bar that can be turned around a fixed point. You can use it to change the place at which you exert a force, the direction of the force, and often its strength.

**load** weight (determined by gravitational force) of an object that a person or machine is trying to move

**mass** amount of matter in an object. It is measured in pounds or kilograms.

**matter** anything that has mass and occupies space

**Newton's first law of motion** states that an object stays at rest or keeps moving in a straight line at a constant speed unless acted on by a force

**Newton's second law of motion**  states that an object tends to accelerate, or speed up, in the direction of a force exerted on it; the greater the force, the more it accelerates, but the more mass the object has, the less it accelerates

**Newton's third law of motion**  states that for every action or force there is an equal and opposite reaction, opposite force

**pressure**  amount of force over a given area

**pulley**  simple machine made of linked wheels that increases the force a person can exert

**reaction**  force that is produced by an action and that is equal and opposite to it.

**resist**  to slow something down; when an object or a material resists something moving, it tends to slow it down. For example, water resists the fall of a diver.

**rigid**  not changing shape

**simple machine**  any device, such as a lever or a pulley, that changes the strength or direction of a force or the place at which it is exerted

**speed**  how fast something moves

**vibration**  fast back–and–forth motion

**volume**  amount of space something takes up

**weight**  measure of force exerted on an object by gravity

# Index

# More Books to Read

Fullick, Anne, and Chris Oxlade. *Science Topics: Forces and Motion*. Chicago: Heinemann Library, 2000.

Lafferty, Peter. *Eyewitness: Force & Motion*. New York: Doris Kingsley Publishing, 2000.

Riley, Peter. *Forces and Movement*. Danbury, Conn.: Franklin Watts, 1998.